THE
CHRISTIAN'S
AMBITION

A COLLECTION OF SPIRITUAL TEACHINGS

JAMES GUNN JR.

THE CHRISTIAN'S AMBITION
By: James Gunn Jr.
Copyright © 2016
GOSPEL FOLIO PRESS
All Rights Reserved

Published by Gospel Folio Press
304 Killaly St. West Port Colborne, ON L3K 6A6

ISBN: 9781927521854

Cover design by Danielle Robins

All Scripture quotations from the
King James Version unless otherwise noted.

Printed in Canada

FORWARD

The Christian's Ambition is the title of the first of a number of addresses by our brother James Gunn Jr. which form the contents of this book.

For the most part, these addresses were given at special gatherings for young Christians in the city of Chicago and elsewhere.

Because of the apparent need among young believers, for this type of ministry we were pleased to print the addresses in our *Young People's Bible Class* edition of our weekly Sunday School paper, *Words of Love,* and now send them forth in this form, trusting that the ministry thus given in booklet form may prove as helpful to the Lord's people as it did when given from the platform.   — *The Publishers*

CONTENTS

THE CHRISTIAN'S AMBITION

The English word ambition is derived from a Latin word which means to go both ways to gain a point. It has an evil sense in it, inferring that one can stoop to duplicity to gain his point. Such is the ambition of the world. The word ambition in the language of the New Testament is a noble word which means a love for honour.

This interesting word is only used three times in the New Testament, so let us look at these three references, and learn from them the lofty height of Christian ambition, for they present this to us under three aspects.

Godward • 2 Corinthians 5:1-10

"Wherefore we labour [we are ambitious], *that, whether present or absent, we may be accepted* [well-pleasing] *of him."* (v. 9)

1. The Christian must labour, must be ambitious is the word, to be acceptable to God. The word *"accepted"* means well pleasing. Now this is a word expressing the behaviour of a servant before his master. *"Exhort servants to be obedient unto their own masters, and to please them well in all things"* (Titus 2:9). The Christian is the servant, and Christ the Master whom he must please well in all things. There is a similar word used by the apostle Paul in his prayer for the Colossians 1:10, *"That ye might walk worthy of the Lord unto all pleasing."* The words *"all pleasing"* suggest the thought of anticipating the pleasure of another, and carries with it the idea of doing things in a patronizing manner, as merchants treat their customers. There is no finer example of this than the godly Enoch (Heb. 11:5), who had this testimony that he pleased God. This then ought to be the ambition of every child of God.

2. There is a twofold reason given why we should be ambitious to please God. The one is because of a favour, and the other is because of fear.

(a) The favour: the word *"wherefore"* (v. 9) throws us back on the first part of the chapter. If we have a house prepared for us in heaven, which will be given to us at the return of Christ, and if we know that should we die before this event, we shall be absent from the body, and present with the Lord this should create in us the ambition to serve Him and please Him who so favoured such unworthy ones.

(b) The fear: The conjunction *"for"* (v. 10) links these two statements together. We labour to be well pleasing to Him, because we must appear before the Judgement Seat of Christ. This word "appear" does not only mean that we must be present. It is the very same word that we have in verse 11, *"We are made manifest unto God."* And as we are manifest before Him now (Heb. 4:13), so that the Judgement Seat of Christ, all our life must be made bare, for then the hidden things of darkness will be made manifest even the counsels of the heart.

Manward • Romans 15:15-20
"Yea, so have I strived [I am ambitious] *to preach the gospel, not where Christ was named, lest I should build upon another man's foundation."* (v. 20)

This believer is revealed to us in the Word of God under many aspects. He is a soldier, a servant, a runner, and etc. Among these many aspects there is a very interesting one, the priest.

The word minister used here is the word from which our English word "liturgy" comes, and associates itself with priestly functions J. N. D. renders this verse thus: *"for me to be minister of Christ Jesus to the nations, carrying on as a sacrificial service the* [message of] *glad tidings of God"* (v. 16). This is the highest conception of the Christian ministry, and the apostle here reveals himself as functioning under both aspects of the Christian priesthood. As the royal priest he goes out with the Evangel of God, and as the holy priest he offers up in worship the results of his work in the gospel.

The climax of this portion is reached at verse 20, " *Yea, so* [after this manner] *have I strived* [been ambitious] *to preach the gospel."* He first of all was ambitious to preach the gospel, so that he might have converts to offer back to God. Just as Levi offered the Levites before the Lord for an offering of the children of Israel, that they might execute the service of the Lord (Num. 8:11). Then he was ambitious to be pioneered in gospel work, so that he would not build upon another man's foundation. Thank God for men of modern times who have been similarly inspired. We think of such men as David Livingstone, J. G. Paton, Hudson Taylor, and etc. Now few of us can do this, for most of us are like Apollos or Barnabas. Paul laid the foundation at Corinth, and Apollos built there on (1 Cor. 3). That is what most of us are doing today; nevertheless, we ought to be ambitious to preach Christ successfully, so that we can offer to God the souls won for Him.

Several years ago, a brother invited me to go and preach the gospel with him in a school house in the district where a number of his relatives lived, and in doing so he said, "I have been not only deeply exercised about my relatives, but also about myself, for I have been saved for thirty years, and I have never had the joy of pointing a soul to Christ." The brother took off time from his business for six weeks, and we went together. I shall not readily forget the evening when he won his first convert—his own nephew. There were others saved at that time, and the heart of the Christian business man was filled with joy. During the years that have intervened my fellow labourer of that series has gone home to heaven, but for some who are still with us it can be said, *"For what is our hope, or joy, or crown of rejoicing? Are not even ye in* the presence of our Lord Jesus Christ at his coming? For ye are our glory and joy" (1 Thess. 2:19-20).

Selfward • 1 Thessalonians 4:11

"Study to be quiet." We generally think that this means to be quiet, silent, but its meaning goes far beyond that. The same word occurs in Luke 23:56 "They rested the Sabbath day." It means to be calm, quiet, restful, or tranquil; to be quiet in spirit rather than quiet in tongue.

There was reason for this exhortation. Paul had taught the young believers at Thessalonica that Jesus was coming again, but after Paul had left them some of their numbers passed away, and they began to fret, fearing that those who had died would have no part in the rapture of the Church, and so they were all disquieted and worried; therefore the apostle says, "Be ambitious to be quiet, as I am." He seems to say to them in their trouble, "Still yourselves and I will fully explain the matter," and this he does in chapter four.

We are living in days of trouble, the hearts of men are failing them, and things in the world would naturally upset the child of God; therefore, we must be ambitious to be quiet and calm. No matter what happens in the home, in the assembly, in the country where we live, or in the world, the child of God should not get into a panic, but with godly self-control study to be quiet and restful in the Lord.

While others in the world may be ambitious to gain for themselves a name and fame, may we only be ambitious to please God, preach Christ, and always be quiet and restful.

THE BLESSEDNESS OF COMMUNION

SONG OF SOLOMON 2:8-17

Very graphically there is brought before us in this portion the visit of the Lover to His Love. This is a picture that all those who are truly the Lord's should readily understand. The lofty heights and characteristic purity of warm love are used to bring before us a lesson in the intimacy of communion between the Lord and Israel, and between Christ and His Church.

In looking at this precious picture and in applying its teaching to ourselves let us consider:

The Barrier • Song of Solomon 2:8, 17

It will be seen from these verses that the mountains of the Bether had come in between the Bridegroom and His Bride. "Bether" means separation, so in plain language, they had been separated, and some obstacle now stood between them. In this same regard it can alas be said that the mountains of spiritual Bether often come between us and our heavenly Bridegroom.

Peter had three falls which clearly illustrate this; first he fell before his Lord, a fall that resulted from pride (Matt. 16:21-23); second, he fell before the world through fear (Matt. 26:67-75); lastly, he fell before his brethren because of his insincerity (Gal. 2:11-14). How often pride, fear, and insincerity come between the blessed Lord Jesus and our souls.

The Barrenness • Song of Solomon 2:10-11

The Bride it is plain to see during this period of separation from her Beloved was resting lazily in a scene of winter. All at this time resulted in fruitlessness and departure. This is always the consequence of separation from our Lord through anything.

The sad story of the nation of Israel is brought before us in a similar way in Isaiah 5:1-7. A vineyard has been planted, but it did not bring forth any fruit, and the result of this barrenness was divine judgement, so let us take care that we bring forth to His glory more fruit. *"For whom the Lord loveth he chasteneth, and scourgeth every son whom he receiveth"* (Heb. 12:6).

The Beloved

Apparently while the Bride was in this sad condition her Beloved bounded over the mountains of separation, and as He came He spoke; the Bride on hearing His voice recognized it, and exclaimed: *"The voice of my beloved!"* (v. 8). Do we always thus recognize the voice of our Beloved Lord? At sometime in the past we heard that voice speaking to us the words of divine forgiveness as He did to one of old (John 8:11), and we shall hear that voice again in the future when He comes for His own (John 5:28-29), but do we hear and heed it now?

The Blessedness

It is very noticeable that as soon as the Bridegroom comes all the scene of winter is changed into a scene of Spring: *"For, lo, the winter is past, the rain is over and gone; The flowers appear on the earth; the time of the singing of birds is come, and the voice of the turtle is heard in our land"* (vv. 11-12).

What a change! Many souls which have wandered away from the Lord have experienced the truth of these word pictures. During their period of backsliding they have passed through a spiritual winter time, but on their return to the Lord it was like the return of Spring, and the many enjoyable features of Spring might well illustrate the many blessings they enjoyed, some of which are enumerated here.

Let us look more carefully at the details of these blessings that belong to those who know the intimacy of sweet communion with the Lord, and listen to the voice of this Infinite Lover as He speaks to and about His Bride.

1. **Her person:** *"My Love"* this is what the Bride is then to the Bridegroom. *"My Fair One"* this is what He has made her in herself (v. 13).

2. **Her place:** *"in a clift of the rock"* (Ex. 33:22). This intimates the eternal security of the believer. The believer in the Lord Jesus Christ like David is upon the Rock (Ps. 40:2), and like Moses he is hidden in the Rock (Ex. 33:22); therefore he will never call upon the rocks to fall upon him to hide him from the wrath of the Lamb (Rev. 6:16).

3. **Her privilege:** To ascend by the stairs into His presence. We who are the people of God have free access if we only avail ourselves of it. *"Having therefore, brethren, boldness to enter into the holiest by the blood of Jesus, By a new and living way, which he hath consecrated for us, through the veil, that is to say, his flesh; Let us draw near with a true heart in full assurance of faith"* (Heb. 10:19-20, 22). *"Them...that come unto God by him"* (Heb. 7:25).

   We can ascend higher on these stairs, we can draw nearer through this way, we can come unto God by Him.

4. **His portion:** *"Let me see thy countenance, let me hear thy voice; for sweet is thy voice, and thy countenance is comely"* (v. 14). We are often more occupied with what blessings we obtain from communion with the Lord rather that what He obtains through communion. From these words we see that He greatly desires our fellowship because it is to Him a source of delight and pleasure.

5. **Her peril:** *"Take us the foxes, the little foxes that spoil the vines"* (v. 15). Here is the voice of the Bridegroom. He will aid us in the removal of those things that hinder fellowship with God. How blessed to think that He helps to remove these things Himself. He as our High Priest holds in His hands the snuffers and the tongs with which He trims our lamp of testimony (Ex. 25:38-40). As the Priest He trims our lamp, and as the

husbandman He prunes our branches (John 15:2), and as our Lord He chastises us (Heb. 12:6), so that we might yield the peaceable fruit of righteousness.

The Burden

The bride now tells us that they are truly one, *"My beloved is mine, and I am his"* (v. 16) and in verse 17 she addresses herself to her Bridegroom and to paraphrase her language she says "Until our marriage-day break, and these shadows give place to a truer substance, come often." This nocturnal visit had been so sweet that she desires more and more. May we be possessed of the same spirit, and seek more intimate fellowship with our Lord in view of that day when we shall see Him face to face.

THE DIVINE INFLUENCE OF THE BIBLE

DANIEL 9:1

There is a proverb that states that the pen is mightier than the sword, and in this there is much truth, because books have influenced the minds of thousands either for good or bad.

In South America the people used to ask us to explain the great moral, social and industrial differences between North and South America. There was no use of arguing this out from the stand point of races—Latin and Anglo Saxon, because that offers no solution to the problem. Here is my explanation: In South America Rome landed with a crucifix in one hand and a sword in the other. It was a question of bow or die. In North America the Pilgrim Fathers landed with a Bible in their hands and a prayer in their hearts. Even though men may not now seek to acknowledge it the Bible has greatly influenced both the United States and Canada.

I want to speak to you of the influence of the Word of God not over a nation, but over one man and as we look at this may we as individuals also be influenced by the constant practice of the reading of the Bible. The reading of the Scriptures has brought comfort, help, and instruction to men in every circumstance of life. In the Old Testament we see the man Daniel with his books in the palace, and in the New Testament we see the apostle Paul with his books in the prison (2 Tim. 4:13).

Daniel

There is no more thrilling story to be found anywhere than the story of the prisoner of war who became the prime minister of the land of his captivity. Daniel we know to be a man of purpose, prayer, and progress.

Daniel's Bible

1. From the passage that we have read we learn something about the Bible that Daniel had. It was not as large as ours, but he possessed and used part of our Old Testament. He had the books of Moses (v. 13), and also the writings of Jeremiah, and these he loved and used. It has been suggested by some that Daniel is the author of the 119th Psalm, and if this be true we can learn from it something of his estimation of the Holy Scriptures.

2. He believed them to be inspired of God. Notice what he calls them, *"The Word of the Lord"* (v. 2). They had come from the mouth of the Lord. *"All Scripture is given by inspiration of God"* (2 Tim. 3:16), that is all Scripture is God breathed.

3. This word of the Lord comes to Daniel by human instrumentality. It was the word of the Lord which came to Jeremiah, and was written down by him. Holy men of God spoke as they were moved by the Holy Ghost (2 Pet. 1:21). God has given us in the Bible a divine message by human hands.

    Another has used a very apt illustration of this: In the beginning God made man out of the dust of the earth. The human form lay there, but it was the form and nothing else. Then He breathed into man the breath of life and man became a living soul. Now it is just so with our Bible. It has a cover, paper, human words, sentences, paragraphs, and etc.—a human form indeed, but God has breathed into it the breath of God and it has come become a living book.

4. Daniel understood his Bible. He understood by books. The fact that he mentions books in the plural suggests

that he compared one with another. He was a thoughtful and diligent reader, and consequently he understood.

Many read their Bibles out of a sense of duty, and therefore do not profit, but there are others like Daniel who read to understand. They compare spiritual things with spiritual.

Daniel's Prayer

The effect of the reading of these inspired words upon Daniel is given us in verse three. Daniel falls upon his face before God. Picture this scene of Daniel upon his knees reading his Bible and praying to his God. Such a sight surely enrages the devil, and yet brings delight to the heart of God. God only knows and eternity alone will tell what has been accomplished by men who kneel before an open Bible in prayer.

1. The word of the Lord read by Daniel first of all governed his attitude Godward. This is seen in the two expressions *"prayer and supplication."* Prayer is a general word; supplication is the specific word. Prayer embraces my whole address to God, supplication refers to the petitions I express in that prayer. Many precious promises in this regard have been left to us. Think of this one, *"Whatsoever ye shall ask the Father in my name, he will give it you"* (John 16:23).

2. This reading also governs his attitude selfward as we see in the last three expressions: fasting, sackcloth, and ashes. Fasting is self-denial and sackcloth and ashes self-abasement. The reading of the Holy Scriptures leads Daniel on the one hand to appeal to God and on the other to abandon self. Now if we read our Bibles in the fear of God it will effect us in the very same way.

Daniel's Vision

What happened to this man who knew of the power of the Bible and the power of prayer?

1. God came into his life in a very unusual, yet in a very spectacular way (vv. 20-21). Do we want the Lord to come into our lives in an unusual way? I know that Gabriel will not be sent with any special message, but I am convinced of this that if we spent more time upon our knees before an open Bible unusual things would happen. We would enjoy His presence in an unusual way. We have fallen into the rut of usual things—the usual Bible reading, the usual prayer meeting. Now thank God for these, but let us strive after great things, unusual things.

2. There are two outstanding men in the Bible, one in the Old Testament the other in the New Testament which were specially loved of God—Daniel (v. 23), and John (John 19:26). It seems strange that these two men beloved in a special way by the Lord were the men chosen to write the two great books of prophecy, Daniel and Revelation. I think the secret of being so loved was this, they loved and used the Book and they loved to pray to the Author of that Book.

3. Daniel was taken into divine secrets. God could trust this man upon his knees before an open Bible, and so He told him that the seventy years Judah's captivity under the Gentiles was just an illustration of seventy weeks of years of Gentile rule and oppression. I am not here going into the significance of Daniel's seventy week, I merely mention them to show that divine secrets are given to men upon their knees in prayer before an open Bible.

4. Here God takes Daniel in spirit and in vision to the days of Christ and to Calvary. That is a strong reason why we should read our Bible in a prayerful attitude. Daniel thereby learnt about Christ and His work upon the cross. The Messiah the Prince shall come (v. 25), the Messiah shall be cut off (v. 26), the Messiah in His death shall finish the transgression, make an end

of sin, make reconciliation, and bring in everlasting righteousness.

It is no wonder then that Daniel never forgot this time when he read those books and prayed to his God. His mind was so deeply impressed that he mentions the very year in which it took place (v. 2). May we know more of the blessedness of reading and praying in the presence of our God.

SPIRITUAL DEVELOPMENT

COLOSSIANS 1:9-14

As we read the letters of the apostle Paul we feel that we are really watching him in his labours for the Master. We see him on the old Roman roads as he journeys from place to place with the gospel, we watch him and listen to him as he takes his seat in the synagogue and reads the Scriptures and reasons with the Jews. We sit among the philosophers of old on Mars hill and hear him as he directs the minds and hearts To The Unknown God (Acts 17:22-23). And in chapter one of his Colossian epistle, we step within the prison door at Rome, and behold a man with chains on arms and legs kneeling upon the pavement bowed in prayer. Let us listen to his prayer, for in it we have the desire of his heart for the Colossians. He prays for their spiritual progress. He hopes that they may grow in grace and in the knowledge of their Lord and Saviour Jesus Christ (2 Pet. 3:18).

Let us look at this subject under several headings:

The Measure of Spiritual Growth

This may be seen in the repetition of the little word *"all."* *"All wisdom"*; *"all pleasing"*; *"Strengthened with all might"*; *"unto all patience."* (vv. 9-11). He desired to find in them a full measure of these Christian graces. It was for full development and perfect maturity that Paul prayed; no partial growth did he wish to see.

In spite of the fact Paul knew that on earth he himself could not reach this; he endeavoured to attain to the state of the resurrection by fellowship with Christ *"That I might know Him, and the power of His resurrection, and the fellowship of His suffering, being made conformable unto His death; if by any means I might attain unto the resurrection of the dead"* (Phil. 3:10-11), and

21

he rebuked the Hebrews for their spiritual immaturity. *"Ye are dull of hearing. For when for the time ye ought to be teachers, ye have need that one teach you again which be the first principles of the oracles of God; and are become such as have need of milk, and not of strong meat"* (Heb. 5:11-12), and also the Corinthians, *"And I, brethren, could not speak unto you as unto spiritual, but as unto carnal, even as unto babes in Christ. I have fed you with milk, and not with meat: for hitherto ye were not able to bear it, neither yet now are ye able. For ye are carnal,"* (1 Cor. 3:1-4). Immaturity in the physical body is a sad thing, and immaturity of mind is a sadder thing, but I think to God the saddest thing of all is a spiritual immaturity. God's desire for us all is full growth.

The Means of Spiritual Growth

In the language of the apostle here there can be seen a twofold request: First, *"that ye might be filled"* (v. 9). Second, *"that ye might walk"* (v. 10). It will be noticed that, the first is unseen while the second is seen; one is private and the other is public; one is the cause and the other is the effect. It is the first of these that really shows the true means of spiritual growth. Let us notice three factors in the acquisition and the operation of the divine will in the Christian. Being *"filled with the knowledge of his will"* (v. 9). That is apprehending the will of God as revealed in the Scriptures. *"In all wisdom"* (v. 9). I judge this means that I must not only know the will of the Lord, but that I must also know its connection to my life and particular circumstances. It is a question of knowing His will and also where it fits. Then we read *"spiritual understanding"* (v. 9). Now this may mean the applying of God's will to my life and ways. These three can be illustrated by Solomon's workmen engaged on the construction of the temple. First, they had to quarry the stones they possessed by taking them out from among all the others. Now that is like the acquisition of knowledge. Second, they were measured for a particular place in the temple, and cut and shaped until they met the specifications, to make sure that they would fit into these places. Last of all, the stones were taken to the temple, and placed in the position where they belonged; they were applied to the building. The second of these reminds us of wisdom and the last one of understanding. As the people of God, to grow in grace, we must through knowledge acquire the will of God, and through wisdom determine just where it fits into our daily life, and then through understanding we must apply it there.

In writing to the Romans the apostle Paul says, *"Be not conformed to this world: but be ye transformed by the renewing of your mind, that ye may prove what is the good and perfect will of God"* (Rom. 12:2). So, then, one learns the will of God not only by the reading of His word, but also by the renunciation of the world.

The Manifestation of Spiritual Growth

" That ye might walk worthy of the Lord" (v. 10). Our spiritual growth is manifest in our walk. The manner of my life is the effect of my knowledge of the will of God.

To what extent am I to walk worthy of the Lord? *"Unto all-pleasing"* (v. 10). Dr. Moule renders this expression "unto every anticipation of His will." This may be illustrated thus: A child dutifully does what his father asks him, and thus please him; but then the child on some occasions anticipated the father's wish and goes and does somethings without being asked, it thereby pleases the father to a much greater extent.

In how many ways is this progressive walk of the child of God to be seen?

1. **In service:** *"Being fruitful in every good work"* (v. 10)
2. **In knowledge:** *"Increasing in the knowledge of God"* (v. 10).
3. **In experience:** *"Strengthened with all might, according to his glorious power, unto all patience and longsuffering with joyfulness"* (v. 11). Strength is required in the every day experiences of life, and it will be given by God unto all patience amidst surrounding circumstances. Patience struggles but endures; long suffering endures without struggling and joyfulness endures and glorifies in

suffering. These are only to be seen in those that have grown in grace and in the knowledge of our Lord and Saviour Jesus Christ, as in the apostle Paul who wrote, *"And not only so, but we glory in tribulation"* (Rom. 5:3).

4. **In gratitude:** *"Giving thanks unto the Father, which hath made us meet to be partakers of the inheritance of the saints in light: Who hath delivered us from the power of darkness, and hath translated us into the kingdom of his dear Son: In whom we have redemption through his blood, even the forgiveness of sins"* (vv. 12-14). Every day the Christian's heart should be filled with gratitude to God. It will be noticed that by inverting the order of things in verse 12 and 14 we have an ascent from lower to higher plains. Forgiveness of sins; redemption through His blood; translation into the kingdom of His dear Son, and participation in the inheritance of the saints in light. No wonder we should be thankful to our God.

May we henceforth be no more children, but may we grow in grace and in the knowledge of our Lord and Saviour Jesus Christ, and may this spiritual development be seen in our walk before God, our brethren and the world.

INSIDE THE VEIL &
OUTSIDE THE CAMP

HEBREWS 10:16-25 & HEBREWS 13:10-16

In the day of the Hebrew saints God had a place and a glorious Person around which He gathered them, and through His fatherly care these have been preserved for all believers unto this day, and so the Holy Spirit exhorts Christians not to forsake the assembling of themselves together (v. 25) for there is in individual living the holy privilege of passing inside the veil and going outside the camp, even so these joys are the portion of all collective gatherings of saints which own the Lordship of Christ. Lest this statement be misunderstood let it be asserted that only those who know in experimental living what it is to pass inside the veil and live outside the camp have any right to enjoy these holy functions in the gatherings of the people of God.

On fears that there are among the assemblies of God's people those who in the collective capacity profess to go into His presence and out to His Person, and yet they know very little of the power of these sacred things in everyday living.

Let us the more carefully examine these two great passages from the epistle (Read Heb. 10:16-25).

The correct understanding of this portion lies in the meaning of the word "veil". When it is said, "Through the veil," most regard the words following, "That is to say, His flesh," as explanatory, but elsewhere in Scripture the veil is regarded as that which keeps man from God. In Eden man veiled himself from God behind fig leaves and trees, and the hindrance then placed by man between his soul and God was maintained both in the tabernacle and the temple. The humanity of Christ is nowhere set before us as a veil between God and man but rather the very opposite.

"No man hath seen God at any time, the only begotten Son,

which is in the bosom of the Father, he hath declared [to make-known to reveal] *him"* (John 1:18).

God *"Hath in these last days spoken unto us by* [in] *his Son"* (Heb. 1:2).

It seems, therefore, more natural from the standpoint of spiritual interpretation to associate the word "flesh" with the word "way" showing that it is Christ incarnate that is the way through the veil of hindrance. Conybeare and Howson render it thus: *"By a new and living way, which he hath consecrated for us, through the veil, that is to say, his flesh"* (Heb. 10:20).

The word, *"therefore"* in verse 19 points backward to verse 18 where Christ is presented to us in His perfect humanity as the sin-offering; while verse 21 points up ward to Christ in His humanity as the great high priest. The first presents the ground of my passing through the veil, the second the means of passing through the veil.

In this passage from chapter 10 we have three exhortations of the Holy Spirit and mention made of three Christian graces in which the three fold attitude of the believer is presented with considerable detail.

The Exhortations

It will be noticed that there are three of these all beginning with the phrase, *"let us"*. The first governs my attitude Godward; the second my attitude worldward, and the third my attitude Churchward. As we dwell within the veil our whole life will be properly governed and controlled.

The Graces

In looking at these three exhortations it will be seen that one particular grace is attached to each. To the first it is faith (v. 22); to the second it is hope (v. 23); and to the last it is love (v. 24).

Within the veil is the place where Christian graces grow. There are many tropical plants that we can admire and enjoy here in these northern parts, not because we can grow them in our gardens, for there they would die, but we can grow them with special care in a greenhouse.

Faith, hope, and love are flowers from another climate, yea, from heaven itself, and they will only grow inside the veil.

The Attitudes

These are Godward, worldward, and Churchward:

1. **Godward:** *"Let us draw near with a true heart in full assurance of faith"* (Heb. 10:22). This is the intimacy of faith, and does not point to the faith of salvation, but faith in a ready acceptance before God through the high-priestly work of Christ.

   Through that work of His I can draw near to God, and the intimacy and nearness with the Lord is the result of my faith in that work.

   What a precious sight before the eye of God it must be to see a collective body of believers, whether large or small, in which every soul appreciates by faith their complete acceptance with God through the priestly ministry of Christ, and passes with holy boldness through that new and living way into His divine presence to worship Him there.

2. **Worldward:** Faith links me with the cross; hope connects me with the glory. By faith I fulfill His request, *"this do in remembrance of me"* (Luke 22:19); through hope I await the fulfillment of His promise *"till I come"* (Luke 19:13).

   "The confession of our hope" (Heb. 10:23) is simply this: I am waiting for Christ and I expect all the glories of the future to be mine in Him; since that is true, I own that here and now I am a stranger and a pilgrim with no continuing city. Hope in Christ causes me to witness before the world that I am not of it although I may be

found at present in it. Truly Moses of old is a remarkable example of practical hope.

3. **Churchward:** In our day we use the word "provoke" in an evil sense. Almost exclusively it is used as synonymous with to exasperate, but its original meaning was to arouse or to excite. Let us excite one another to love, would express the meaning of this verse. This is the only spiritual excitement that we are enjoined to practice. And as believers are excited to love they do not forsake the assembling of themselves together. Love would thus result in an intimate and steady fellowship in the Church.

We have heard believers severely criticize the assembly where they are for its lack of love. Those who have done so have forgotten that loves begets love. I must not expect everybody in the assembly to love me. My duty is to love every brother and sister in the assembly, and thus excite love in the hearts of others towards me.

Before leaving this portion of the epistle let us consider the forceful exhortation given to us in verse 25. We cannot afford to neglect the gatherings of God's people for it is there that the joy of the passing within the veil in the company of devoted souls is ours, and with them in the divine precincts we can worship by faith, witness to hope, and provoke love.

The verb assembly found in this 25 verse occurs in only one other instance in the New Testament, *"Now we beseech you, brethren by the coming of our Lord Jesus Christ, and by our gatherings together* [assembling together] *unto Him"* (2 Thess. 2:1). And if we may use this instance as an illustration we suggest that our gathering together in assembly capacity should be complete, for as at His coming all His saints will be gathered to Him, even so now all, or nearly possible all, the saints should be in the assembly meetings.

Let us consider together the three contrasts that are brought before us in Hebrews 13:10-16.

The People Contrasted

"We," in this word the writer associates himself with the others, his readers, who profess to be true Christians; therefore, in this word we have all Christians represented. We Christians have an altar.

"They," in this word we have revealed to us a body of people, who are characterized by the fact they served the tabernacle. It is not at all difficult to determine who are meant. They were Jews and proselytes, that still held to the old order of the Levitical ritualism.

The Provisions Contrasted

1. **The Altar:** For an earthly people God provided the tabernacle, but for a heavenly people He provided an Altar. Now, this Altar is Christ in all His solitary dignity, as will be seen from verse 15, *"By him therefore let us offer the sacrifice of praise to God."*

2. **The Tabernacle:** This building and the priesthood connected with it was at the first of divine institution, and so was the temple. The later was the permanent form of that which had been temporary. Because of the corruption of man God was forced to leave it entirely. It was of course only a transitory thing at the best, because it appealed more to the eye than to the spirit. In connection with the tabernacle we have, rules and regulations, furniture and images, besides priests and vestments and musical instruments.

The Places Contrasted

Here we have the tabernacle and the camp in contrast to the nameless place outside the camp. The tabernacle and the camp speak of Judaism in all its forms, religiously and politically; apart from these altogether, the Christian meets to worship and serve His God, *"Wherefore Jesus also, that he might sanctify the people with his own blood, suffered without the gate"* (Heb. 13:12).

Christ our sin-offering was altogether too pure, too holy to suffer within the walls of apostate, polluted Jerusalem, so He suffered and He died outside, and this He did not only to save us, but to separate us from all the defilement of the world in all its aspects.

Today we have not so much trouble with Judaism itself; but we have in our lands what might be called Christianized Judaism for surely that is the true character of carnal religion with its rules and creeds, order, choirs, clergy, vestments and etc., but as Christ turned His back upon old Judaism, and suffered without the gate; even so, the Christian sharing His reproach turns his back upon this imitation and gathers simply in the name of the Lord Jesus enjoying the fulfillment of His precious promise, *"For where two or three are gathered together in my name, there am I in the midst of them"* (Matt. 18:20). *"Let us go forth therefore unto him without the camp, bearing his reproach"* (Heb. 13:13).

The writer Paul, was already outside, and so were the majority of his readers. What does he mean? Simply this, we must not only go forth once, but we must continue to go forth in heart. We are not only to be positionally outside the camp, but we likewise are to be conditionally outside the camp.

The Altar

There are two uses of the Altar mentioned here. In verse 10 the Christian eats at the Altar, whereas in verse 15 he worships at the Altar.

It is the sin-offering that is referred to here and this view of the work of Christ speaks here of identification, and fellowship, for as the priests of old ate their portion of the sin-offering within the court of the tabernacle (Ex. 6:26; Ex. 10:16-20); even so, we, on the ground of our Sin-Offering—Christ, fellowship with God in the position of nearness.

Now according to verse 15 we worship and sacrifice through Him our praise and property. In writing to the Romans the apostle adds to these our person (Rom. 12:1).

May we, therefore, separated from the Christianized Judaism worship at our Altar, and place our all upon it for God.

Living the rest of our lives here inside the veil with God, and outside the camp with Christ. The days of opportunity here are quickly passing, may we by His grace so live that we may not be ashamed when He comes to gather together the elect in one when we shall go in to go no more out forever.

JEHOVAH NISSI OR MORE THAN CONQUERORS

EXODUS 17:8-16

Many young believers have been plunged into distress because of the internal struggle which they find in process every day. Before they were saved they enjoyed comparative rest. The reason for that is simply stated in Romans 6:20: *"For when ye were the servants of sin, ye were free from righteousness"*. There was no conflicting element within to combat the lusts of the flesh, consequently like the apostle Paul they had discovered, *"for what I would, that do I not; but what I hate, that do I"* (Rom. 7:15). *"The flesh lusteth against the Spirit, and the Spirit against the flesh: and these are contrary the one to the other"* (Gal. 5:7).

The spiritual war is typified for us in this portion of the book of Exodus.

There are four leading people in this war which has been recorded for our instruction, Israel, Amalek, Moses and Joshua. Let us prayerfully consider them.

Israel

1. The Israelites were the descendants of Jacob as Amalek was of Esau. Jacob was sufficiently spiritual and wise to appreciate the value of the birthright; whereas Esau was so fleshly and carnal that he despised it. So the words of the Lord are recorded, *"Jacob have I loved, but Esau have I hated"* (Rom. 9:13). Therefore, it is readily seen that Israel is the beloved and favoured of God, and for this cause alone Amalek would hate him.

2. The whole congregation had experienced the might power of God in redemption. They knew that they

were safe through the blood of the paschal lamb, and they also rejoiced in the liberty which God wrought for them by His power at the Red Sea. Theirs was the sweetness, abundance, satisfaction, rest, and refreshment afforded by the provisions of God for His people in the wilderness.

3. Israel at this particular time of their history appears to be in fairly good condition for contrary to the general thing in recording outstanding events, the Holy Spirit had no murmuring nor complaining to reveal.

By putting these three things together we find Israel a type of the spiritual man. He is chosen, favoured, and redeemed, and he rejoices in the provisions given him by God.

Amalek

Amalek was the grandson of fleshly Esau (Gen. 36:12), and for that reason he would not look favourably upon Jacob's descendants.

1. *"Because the Lord hath sworn that the Lord will have war with Amalek from generation to generation"* (Ex. 17:16). From this marginal rendering we see that Amalek had no love for God nor the people of God.

2. Saul's incomplete obedience to this revelation of God is seen in 1 Samuel 15. Saul was a man of the flesh, and he spared Agag the king of the Amalekites. The typical teaching of 1 Samuel 28:18 is very, very solemn, and how fearfully and literally it was fulfilled is revealed to us in 2 Samuel 1. Saul spared Amalek and Amalek slew Saul. Therefore, while in Israel we see the spiritual man; in Amalek we have a type of the fleshly, carnal man, and according to Galatians 5:17 *"the flesh lusteth against the Spirit, and the Spirit against the flesh: and these are contrary the one to the other"*. It is a war to all generations, and as in the case of Saul, either we must overcome the flesh or the flesh will overcome us.

Moses

This wonderful servant of God, as we have seen is a precious type of Christ. We have seen him in death, burial and resurrection, and now again he stands before us as another type of our Lord.

1. Moses ascends the hill, and from thence he watches the battle. Christ likewise has ascended on high, and from thence He sees us in our struggle and war with the flesh.

2. He lifted up his hands in intercession with the rod of God. That rod to the foe of Israel was the rod of judgement, but to Israel it was the rod of deliverance. How gratifying to Joshua and his men to know that for the overthrow of the enemy, and for the deliverance of Israel the rod of God's power was extended.

3. Aaron and Hur supported the tired hands of Moses. Aaron was the head of the priestly family, and Hur was a member of the tribe of Judah, the kingly tribe (Ex. 31:2); therefore, we learn by this type that Christ is sustained in His work because of His priestly office and kingly dignity (Heb. 4:14). And unlike Moses, His hands never wax weary.

Joshua

1. This is the Hebrew name for Jesus and I am sure that we have a picture of Christ also. In Moses we have a picture of Christ in the heavens interceding for us at God's right hand, but in Joshua down in the valley we have a picture of Christ in our hearts empowering us by His Holy Spirit (Col. 1:27).

2. The sword: This was Joshua's only weapon. We also have a sword, the Word of God (Eph. 6:17). This was the weapon used by our Lord in conflict with the devil (Matt. 4:1-11). The Word of God used in the power of the indwelling Christ means victory.

THE CHRISTIAN'S AMBITION

The Battle

Here we have a complete picture of the battle. Israel, the spiritual man, and Amalek, the carnal man are at war. Moses a type of Christ in the heavens intercedes for Israel, and Joshua, a type of Christ in the heart, empowers and leads on to victory.

1. The start of the battle: We learn this from Deuteronomy 25:17-19. Amalek *"smote the hindmost...even all that were feeble."* And so it is in the spiritual realm. Those who follow afar off like Peter, and those who like the Corinthians are weak and sickly are his easy prey.

2. The manner of the battle: *"go out, fight"* (v. 9). There are no half-way measures here. The command is fight, and that does not mean target practice, but war.

3. The close of the battle: On the field of Waterloo there stands to mark the place of victory a huge mound surmounted with the Belgic Lion, and here and there may be seen monuments where heros such as Picton and Ponsonby fell. The victorious Israelites erected not a monument, but an altar, and it was not to perpetuate the remembrance of their own prowess but to ascribe all the glory to God.

May we in all our successes render all praise and glory to Him who gives us the victory through our Lord Jesus Christ, and let us ever stand under His banner, Jehovah Nissi.

SEVEN COMMENDABLE
FEATURES OF AN
ASSEMBLY OF GOD

1 CORINTHIANS 1:1-17

The lessons taught us in this epistle are lessons more of instruction than example. We should learn through the failures of others not to follow their bad examples; therefore, the Holy Spirit would teach us more about what Corinth should have been than what she really was.

The Character of the Assembly

1. **The character of an assembly is clearly revealed in the expression "Church of God."** This infers at least two things. First, the Church of God at Corinth was of God in its origin. It really existed because God was its designer and founder. This later He did through the apostle Paul (1 Cor. 3:10). Secondly, it was of God because it belonged to Him (1 Cor. 3:9). This Church was His and therefore belonged to no one else, either leader or party.

2. **Church:** The original word *ecclesia* means called out, and this meaning is clearly illustrated by the expression *"The church in the wilderness"* (Acts 7:38). The word church is here applied to Israel as a congregation.

    Truly the congregation of Israel was a called out one. They had been delivered from Egypt by blood and power, and of them Balaam said, *"lo, the people shall dwell alone, and shall not be reckoned among the nations"* (Num. 23:9). Israel was a people called out from Egypt and separated from all nations around them. This then is true of God's people today (2 Cor. 6:14-18).

3. **The dual use of the expression Church of God:** The apostle Paul in this very epistle uses this expression in

two different ways. Look at 1 Corinthians 10:32, *"Give none offence neither to Jew nor to Gentile, nor to the Church of God."* Here we learn that God divides humanity into three groups and one of those groups is the Church of God in its world wide aspect, composed of every believer in the Lord Jesus Christ.

Look now at 1 Corinthians 1:2 *"Unto the church of God which is at Corinth."* This is not the Church in the world, but the Church in a certain locality. These two aspects of the Church have been called the universal aspect of the Church. Now from the comparison of Scripture we know that there are some things true of the Universal Church which are not true of the Local Church, and there are some things true of the Local Church which are not true of the Universal Church. Notwithstanding this, both should be alike in character—a gathering of called out ones in separation from the world. In this respect the Local Church should be a miniature of the Universal—a smaller replica of the mighty whole.

The Membership of the Assembly

1. *"...to them that are sanctified in Christ Jesus, called to be saints"* (v. 2). The words "to be" are in italics and are therefore better omitted, when this is done the meaning is simplified. The Corinthians were called saints because they were sanctified. Sanctification means separation, and there are at least three aspects of this truth in the New Testament; the positional, the progressive, and the cumulative. In my judgement it is the positional aspect that is referred to here, and this aspect is described in Hebrews 2:11, *"For both he that sanctifieth and they who are sanctified are all of one".* That is they are all of one nature. Those who are sanctified in Christ Jesus, and made partakers of His nature are called saints or holy ones.

2. It is well to notice that he addresses the Church at Corinth as composed of only sanctified ones, although

later on he says to them, *"Examine yourselves, whether ye be in the faith; prove your own selves. Know ye not your own selves, how that Jesus Christ is in you, except ye be reprobates?"* (2 Cor. 13:5). There were apparently some whom he doubted, but here in his address he takes them on the ground of their profession, and in so doing reveals to us the truth that in a perfectly ordered assembly there should only be those who are sanctified in Christ Jesus. There possibly never has been an assembly where this has been perfectly true; there always have been men creeping in who are ungodly men turning the grace of God into lasciviousness (Jude 4). Nevertheless this is God's standard. A Church of God in any locality should be only composed of those who are sanctified in Christ Jesus called holy.

The Subject of the Assembly

1. *"...all that in every place call upon the name of Jesus Christ our Lord"* (v. 2). The word "to call" used here means, to put a name upon or to surname, as well as to invoke.

In Acts 2:36 we read, *"let all the house of Israel know assuredly, that God hath made the same Jesus, whom ye have crucified, both Lord and Christ"*. God has made Him Lord and all saints in collective capacity should own Him as such, and call Him by that title.

Now what does this imply? Let us look at an example in 1 Peter 3:6, *"Sara obeyed Abraham, calling him lord"*. Now in this portion the verb to call is the same one as is used in 1 Corinthians 1, so that as Sara called Abraham lord, and thereby denoted her submission and obedience to him, the Corinthians should also have done, and so should every Church of God in any locality. He is Lord and His people should be subject to Him.

He is not our Lord alone, but also the Lord of His people everywhere who acknowledge Him as such. He is Lord both theirs and ours.

The great apostle was trying to impress the lordship of Christ upon the hearts of the Corinthians, for they were submitting to others and calling the names of others upon themselves, so Paul in his letters keeps this divine title of Christ before them and sues it sixty-two times in the first epistle and thirty times in the second. These are the epistles of His Lordship in a very special way and sense.

May we truly acknowledge Him as our Lord, and be subject to Him and Him alone.

Endowment

In this portion we have a wonderful unfolding of the truth in regard to spiritual gifts.

1. *"Ye are enriched by Him"* (v. 5). Christ is the source of all spiritual gift. By comparing Ephesians 4:7-11 with Psalm 68 we learn that Christ has captured that which had held men captives, and now in His triumph He distributes the spoils of war as gifts among men, and Corinth had been greatly blessed, so that the apostle says, *"Ye are enriched."*

2. *"ye come behind in no gift"* (v. 7). Literally, "You are behind in not one gift." Now here we have variety, there was not one gift at Corinth by many; all were from Christ but all were not the same. Generally speaking God does not endow one man with all the gifts but some are evangelists, some are pastors, and teachers. Much confusion has resulted at times when men have attempted to use the gift that really belongs to another.

   These gifts all differ, but that is His own order, and so under His lordship these diversified gifts can function in perfect harmony.

3. *"...ye are enriched by him, in all utterance, and in all knowledge"* (v. 5). Literally, "In all discourse and knowledge." These two things must always characterize

the divinely endowed gift or talent—knowledge and utterance; cause and effect. We know therefore do we speak. There must be divine knowledge before there can be divine utterance, and if we have not that God given knowledge we have no right to speak.

The doctrine of the gifts is clearly taught in the epistle of Ephesians and the epistle to the Corinthians. The former is the epistle of the Universal Church, the latter the epistle of the Local Church. I would take it therefore as God's ideal that gifts have been given to the Universal Church to function through the Local Church.

Anticipation

Here we have to expressions, *"the coming of our Lord Jesus"* (2 Thess. 2:1), and *"the day of our Lord Jesus Christ"* (v. 8). The first one points to an event and the second to a period of time.

1. **The event:** His coming, His unveiling for such is the meaning of the word used here. The same word is used in Romans 8:19 in connection with the Sons of God, and there refers to that happy moment when the redeemed will be made manifest before the Universe. But the unveiling of Christ, points to that actual revelation of Christ before the wondering eyes of His own. The appearing of Jesus Christ whom having not seen we love, in whom though now ye see Him, not yet believing, ye rejoice with joy unspeakable (1 Pet. 1:8).

    Face to face with Christ my Saviour,
    Face to face what will it be,
    When with rapture I behold Him,
    Jesus Christ who died for me.

2. **The time:** The day of Christ. There are four days spoken of in the New Testament. Man's Day (1 Cor. 4:3), the present period of time. The day of the Lord (2 Thess. 2:2), that period on earth after the rapture of

the Church, spoken of as the day of the Lord's fierce anger. The day of Christ (Phil. 2:16), that period in heaven between the coming of Christ for His people and the coming of Christ with His people. Then the day of God (2 Pet. 3:12-13), the Eternal state.

Here the apostle reminds the Corinthians that with the coming of Christ there will also be the day of Christ, and consequently the Judgement Seat of Christ, where all our service will be reviewed.

Fellowship

That every child of God can and ought to enjoy fellowship with the Lord there is no doubt, *"our fellowship is with the Father, and with his Son Jesus Christ"* (1 John 1:3). But there is not only individual fellowship, but also collective fellowship which we may enjoy. Of the primitive Christians we read that they continued steadfastly in the apostle's doctrine, and in the fellowship, and in the prayers (Acts 2:42). May we not only enjoy personal, individual fellowship with the Lord but may we also enter into and appreciate collective fellowship among the assemblies of God's people.

Unity

What an appeal we have here for the unity of an assembly of God! That the Church of God at Corinth was sadly divided is very evident. Some were making party heads of men while others were making a party head of Christ.

In this appeal we read three important things: speak the same thing, in the same mind, in the same judgement.

1. **Our thoughts:** the same mind.
2. **Our opinions:** the same judgement.
3. **Our expression:** speak the same thing.

This is a very high standard of unity, but it is God's standard, and all of His divine standards are high. Now we have failed, but God will never lower His standard to suit us, so therefore we must constantly endeavour to attain in some degree at least the standard of our God.

There is a lovely word picture painted here in the words *"perfectly joined together"* (v. 10). In Mark 1:19 the Lord Jesus finds some disciples in a ship mending their nets. Now the word rendered "mending" there is the same word rendered "perfectly joined together" here, and if we put these two passages together we have a picture of an assembly as a fishing net. When the net is torn the fish escape and there is no success, but when the net is mended, perfectly joined together, then men and women will be caught in this Gospel net and brought to Christ. Let us then mend our nets and be perfectly joined together, so that we may be successful fishers of men for Christ.

A CONSECRATED PRIESTHOOD

LEVITICUS 8; EXODUS 29

In the consecration of Aaron and his sons we have revealed to us typically many of the experiences through which a truly consecrated soul must pass. We often use Aaron as a type of Christ, but here he stands in contrast to our Lord, because being only a man it was necessary that atonement be made for his personal sins.

The Washing • Leviticus 8:6

In this washing we have a picture of regeneration, for according to Titus 3:5 we are saved by the washing of regeneration, and not by the works of righteousness which we have done.

1. At this ceremonial consecration we notice that the priests were subjected to entire ablution, though on ordinary occasions they were required, before entering upon their duties, only to wash their hands and feet. It was to these things that the Lord Jesus made reference when He answered Peter in the upper room, *"He that is washed needeth not save to wash his feet, but is clean every whit"* (John 13:10). Thank God for all who know complete cleansing through regeneration, and now only need to wash their feet from defilement contacted on the pathway of life.

2. It is worthy to notice that on this occasion the washing was not done by Aaron although afterwards he was responsible to wash his hands and his feet himself. Here it was all performed by a power and an element apart from himself. How like the work in the regeneration of a soul.

The Clothing • Leviticus 8:7, 13

1. Here we have a picture of justification. They were clothed in robes which fitted them for the presence of God. The antitype of this robe is brought before us in Romans 3:22 *"Even the righteousness of God which is by faith of Jesus Christ unto all and upon all them that believe"*. Just as Moses held out those garments to Aaron and his sons and then put them on, so God holds out His righteousness, but He only puts it on them that believe.

2. What a wonderful picture we have here. Aaron's sons stand clothed in pure white linen with Aaron in their midst in his robes of beauty and glory. It is not difficult to visualize that scene, and it reminds us of another scene, a scene in heaven. *"After this I beheld, and, lo, a great multitude, which no man could number, of all nations, and kindreds, and people, and tongues, stood before the throne, and before the Lamb, clothed with white robes, and palms in their hands"* (Rev. 7:9). The Lamb character of Christ brings before us His priesthood, and the Lion character of Christ reveals to us His kingship. Here He is the glorified Priest in the midst of a redeemed priesthood clothed in pure white linen – those justified from all things by His own blood, and now glorified by His own power.

The Offerings • Leviticus 8:14-22

By these two offerings reconciliation was accomplished. There was first of all a sin offering, which brings before us the work of Christ manward, as it meets the need of the sinner; then there was a burnt offering, which brings before us the work of Christ Godward, as it satisfies all His righteous demands. The wonderful result of these two was reconciliation.

The order here is truly divine. First there is that which speaks of cleansing through regeneration; then there is that which speaks of justification, being clothed in divine righteousness; and now those who were thus regenerated and justified are reconciled, brought nigh to God (1 Pet. 3:18).

The Blood Applied • Leviticus 8:23-26

1. In this we have a picture of redemption. We may look at this, subject in the light of the New Testament in a very simple way. There are at least two aspects of the truth. First, "redemption from"; the saints are redeemed from the curse of the law (Gal. 3:13); from all lawlessness (Tit. 2:14); and from the vain manner of living received from their forefathers (1 Pet. 1:18). But there is another aspect concerning which we often forget, namely, "redemption to." Thou *"hast redeemed us to God by thy blood"* (Rev. 5:9) and this will be the song of the saints in heaven.

2. It is this second aspect that we have foreshadowed here. The blood on the thumb, toe, and ear of the priest, declared not so much that he had been redeemed from Egypt, for that was really accomplished in the death of the paschal lamb (Ex. 12), but that he had been redeemed to God. All his activities were God's by purchased right as seen by the blood on the foot. All his attainments belonged to the Lord for there was blood on the hand and all his intellectual powers belonged to the Lord for there was blood on his head. May we never forget that He has redeemed us body, soul, spirit to our God. We belong to Him by purchase right.

Empty Hands Filled • Leviticus 8:25-29

1. We have come to that part of the chapter that clearly illustrates the true meaning of consecration. Moses took different parts of the ram of consecration, and upon them he placed unleavened bread, unleavened cakes, oiled bread, and a wafer, and he put all upon the hands of the priest. Now this is what it is to be consecrated.

All these things speak of Christ in His sinless person and accomplished work. True consecration to the Lord is therefore having our hands filled to the full with our blessed Lord Jesus Christ, and we need our hands full of Christ in testimony, as we go into the presence of God our hands must be full of Christ in worship.

2.   **The empty hands:** Before I can be consecrated by God my hands must be emptied. God always starts with empty hands. That is where God started with Moses. *"What is that in thine hand? And he said, A rod. And he said, Cast it on the ground"* (Ex. 4:2-3). There Moses appears before God with empty hands, and God put something back into his hands that day that never again really belonged to Moses, but something, that when his hands were filled by it did great things for God. That staff was afterwards called the rod of God.

God started Aaron out in his public work with empty hands, as we see in this chapter.

Saul filled David's hands with armour, and a sword, and David could do nothing, but when his hands were emptied God put a sling in them, and some smooth stones, with which David triumphed over Goliath.

The Holy Spirit says, " *I will therefore that men pray every where, lifting up holy hands, without wrath and doubting"* (1 Tim. 2:8). Here the hands are extended before God to show Him that they are empty of all defilement and are clean.

One evening while speaking to a large gathering of young people the suggestion was made that we might look at our hands to see if they were really empty and clean. One young man, a professing Christian confessed to an elder brother afterwards that on looking at his hands he saw the stains of nicotine, which condemned him in the presence of the Lord. Alas, an examination, of our hands in the light of the sanctuary would figuratively reveal much of self, sin, and the world.

Let us empty our hands of everything that dishonours Him, the pipe, the cards, the novel, and etc., so that we can be again consecrated by the Lord.

3. Notice that *"he put all upon Aaron's hands"* (8:27). Hands in the plural. Both had to be emptied, and then both were filled. Some might like to retain the world in one hand, and then have Christ in the other, but this can never do, for God must have all or nothing.

The Anointing Oil • Leviticus 8:30

This anointing oil speaks to us of the Holy Spirit.

"But the anointing which ye have received of him abideth in you, and ye need not that any man teach you: but as the same anointing teacheth you of all things, and is truth, and is no lie, and even as it hath taught you, ye shall abide in him" (1 John 2:27).

The lesson that we must learn from this is a simple one. The consecrated soul is a spirit taught and guided soul.

Food for the Priests • Leviticus 8:32

These newly consecrated priests are here seen feeding on the sacrifices that speak to us of Christ. They had a satisfying portion from the offerings of their God. As they literally fed on the flesh of those sacrifices, even so we spiritually feed on that divine sacrifice Christ Jesus our Lord, and as we do so we can sing:

Satisfied with Thee Lord Jesus, I am blest;
Peace which passeth understanding, on Thy breast,
No more doubting, no more trembling, Oh! what rest!

Occupied with Thee Lord Jesus, in Thy grace;
All Thy ways and thoughts about me, only trace
Deeper stories of the glories of Thy grace.

THE CHRISTIAN'S AMBITION

Taken up with Thee Lord Jesus, I would be;
Finding joy and satisfaction all in Thee;
Thou the nearest and the dearest unto me.

List'ning for Thy shout Lord Jesus, in the air!
When Thy saints shall rise with joy to meet Thee there,
O what gladness! No more sadness, sin nor care.

AN AUTOBIOGRAPHY OF THE APOSTLE PAUL

PHILIPPIANS 1:12-26

On the shelves of libraries there are many different kinds of books. There are books of science, books of history, books of travel, and books of biography, but among all the different classes of reading matter the autobiography holds a special place of interest; for therein, you read the writer's own experience in his own words; you learn more of his character and ability and you can enter more into his feelings.

In this portion of this chapter, the great apostle to the Gentiles is writing about himself, and there are several chapters that suggest themselves to our minds, as we read his own language.

Paul: A Brother in Christ

Twice over in this short sketch of his experience the apostle speaks of his brethren in Christ. In verse 12 he speaks of the friendly Philippians as brethren in Christ, and in verse 14 he speaks of the friendly ones in Rome as brethren; and, shameful though it was for them, the apostle speaks of some envious ones who preached Christ for strife, as brethren. The large heart of the apostle Paul embraced as a brother every believer in Christ whether they were friendly disposed towards him or otherwise.

The principle thought here is not that of relationship, but rather that of consideration. He knew that he was a brother of them all, but here he wants to play a brother's part. They are anxious and worried about his imprisonment, so he writes to set their minds at ease. How beautifully brotherly consideration shines out in all the life of Paul. Notice especially Philemon (vv. 13-14) where, writing to the brother at Colosse about his fugitive slave he says, *"without thy mind would I do nothing"* (v. 14). May we daily learn to manifest towards our brethren brotherly love and consideration.

Paul: A Prisoner of the Lord

The apostle is in prison at Rome, but while the body is bound the spirit is free. Was the apostle a prisoner of Nero?

Listen to his own words, *"my bonds in Christ"* (v. 13). He uses similar language in writing to Philemon a, *"prisoner of Jesus Christ"* (Eph. 3:1). He was not in prison because of Nero, but, rather because of Christ. What courage fills this servant of the Lord! Has Nero any power over him? Is he at the mercy of this human monster? Look carefully at verses 25-26 where he speaks definitely of his release. *"And having this confidence, I know that I shall abide and continue with you all for your further-ance and joy of faith; That your rejoicing may be more abundant in Jesus Christ for me by my coming to you again"* Surely heavenly courage filled his heart, and strengthened his faith.

The praetorian Prefect, Brutus, into whose custody Paul had been committed (Acts 28:16) died, and Nero the emperor having divorced Octavia and married Poppoas, a Jewish pros-elytess, who had caused her rival Octavia to be murdered and then gloated over the head of her victim, exalted Tegellinus, the chief promoter of the marriage, a monster of wickedness, to the Praetorian Prefect. This unpleasant change does not in anywise effect the confidence of the apostle Paul. His keeper in the prison may be a moral brute, but Paul knows that the God who shut the mouths of the hungry brutes in Babylon long ago, and saved His servant Daniel, can control the blood thirsty brute of Imperial Rome.

There are hundreds of prisoners of the Lord whose free spirits are similarly courageous. Look at that invalid sister who cannot walk, and yet she faces life with boldness and fortitude; and at the blind brother who needs someone to lead him about, and yet his faith is vigorous and fruitful. I know two men, both of them children of God, who have lain in the hospital for years. When you ask the one how he is you generally get several answers "I don't feel at all well." "Nobody cares for me now." "People are only your friends for what they can get out of you, and so I don't feel like seeing anybody today." "I am starved in this place, and the nurses never give one proper care." Etc. But when you cross the ward you see a man that is absolutely helpless; he can neither move hand nor foot, and yet his poor body is constantly trembling. When you ask him how he is, he generally replies "Pretty good, thank you." "I had a lovely dinner today, and that little nurse is so attentive, and poor child she was just run off her feet." Then is it his time to ask questions, "Where have you been preaching since you were here last? Did anyone get converted? How are the wife and children?" To my mind dear brother Ball, for that is his name, is a modern prisoner of Jesus Christ. Prisoner he surely is, unable to move, but then that is to him the Lord's mind, and he quietly submits.

Paul: A Solider of the Cross

Paul was now on the defence as we shall see, but he knew what it was to fight an offensive battle as well.

Two of the greatest battles of ancient history were fought at Philippi. The first was fought by Augustus Caesar and Antony against Brutus and Cassius. When the battle ended in complete defeat for these two they both committed suicide. It was a great victory deciding the fate of the Roman Empire. The second and greater victory was fought for Christ by Paul and Silas against the powers of darkness (Acts 16). It resulted in the entrance of the Gospel into Europe. It was a mighty triumph for these Philippians became the willing captives of Jesus Christ.

There is much to be learned from the expression in verse 17. *"I am set for the defence of the gospel."* He really meant, I am appointed by my superior commander, as a defender of the gospel. Many men have been appointed at different stages of history, to defend their country, so it was with the apostle Paul.

In speaking to this great defender of the gospel we might say to him that instead of being a defender, he actually is a captive—a prisoner of war. And he might reply, You mistake my position, my presence here is a strategic move on the part of the Captain of my salvation and it is working out gloriously: *"the things which happened unto me have fallen out rather unto the furtherance of the gospel"* (v. 12). Paul in everything was absolutely submissive to the Lord. Our lives are only God glorifying to the same proportion that we submit to His will. It matters not whether we are in service or in solitude, submission to His will is what pleases Him.

Paul: The Magnifier of Christ

When at work as a chemist there were from time to time things brought in for examination too small to be seen by the naked eye. These small objects were placed under a microscope, and by the lens of that instrument magnified many times their actual size making it possibly to see and study them. Now that is all the apostle Paul wanted to be—just a lens by which Christ might be magnified. The world did not notice Him; He was considered by most to be insignificant, but in life and in death Paul wanted to enlarge Him before their eyes until they could see His beauty. How like John the Baptist who said, *"He must increase, but I decrease"* (John 3:30). Paul had the glory of Christ and the need of the world at heart, have we? He thought nothing of self. Self-abnegation was a constant study with him. John the Baptist wanted to be only a voice to announce Christ (John 1:23), and Paul wanted to be only a lens to magnify Him.

This has been beautifully illustrated in modern times in the triumphs of John and Betty Stam who were beheaded by the Communists of China in December 1934, for the testimony of Jesus Christ. Brother Stam's last letter is worthy of our perusal.

Tsingteh, An.
Dec. 6, 1934

China Inland Mission
Shanghai

Dear brethern,

My wife, baby and myself are today in the hands of the Communists, in the city of Tsingteh. Their demand is twenty thousand dollars for our release.

All our possessions and stores are in their hands, but we praise God for peace in our hearts, and a meal tonight. God grant you wisdom in what you do, and us fortitude, courage, and peace of heart. He is able and a Wonderful Friend at such a time.

Things happened so quickly this a.m. They were in this city just a few hours after the persistent rumour became alarming, so we could not prepare to leave in time. We were just too late.

The Lord bless and guide you, and for us, may God be glorified whether by life or by death.

In Him,
John C. Stam.

THE CHRISTIAN'S AMBITION

Paul: The Ambitious Ambassador

Let us think of the desire of the apostle, *"having a desire to depart, and to be with Christ"* (v. 23). He longed to loosen his anchor (2 Tim. 4:6), and to set sail for home. He was like an ambassador aboard, weary in work and labour, longing for that time when his period of service would end, and he would be able to leave for home. Now look at the necessity to which he points (v. 24): he sees that he is still needed here and he realizes that his labours are worth while. What will characterize him while he waits and works until his period of office expires, *"For to me to live is Christ"* (v. 21).

In the Incarnation it was God with us; at Calvary it was God for us; at Pentecost it was God in us; but in Christian experience it is God through us. Christianity is Christ, and through us Christ must be seen.

A missionary to India tells of a visit that he paid to a distance village where he thought that the gospel had never been heard. He gathered together a large company and told them the wonderful story of Jesus. How He came from the distant home so beautiful, and how He suffered here among men, and also how He healed the sick and blessed the little children. He also enlarged the fact that He revealed the way to heaven, and he closed his story by telling that Jesus had gone back to His home in heaven. When he had finished a very aged man in the village arose and said, "That man you speak of was here many, many years ago; he came from a comfortable home in a beautiful land across the sea; he brought pills and medicine, and healed our sick ones; He also loved our little children and told us of the way to heaven; but, then as you say, he went away back home to his own beautiful land. To me it seems very strange; you say his name is Jesus, but that is not the name he told us. If I remember correctly he told us that his name was Dr. Bland."

May more of Christ been seen through us, and may we too have that desire of the heart to live Christ.

AN AUTOBIOGRAPHY OF THE APOSTLE PAUL

The apostle has written part of his biography here with paper and pen. Are we aware of the fact that we are writing our biography, not on paper with ink, but on the minds and hearts of others; not in words only, but in attitude, actions, and deeds.

FISHERS OF MEN

JOHN 1:35-51

After the miraculous draught of fishes (Luke 5:1-11) Peter fell down before Jesus and said, *"Depart from me; for I am a sinful man, O Lord"* (Luke 5:8). Peter felt himself utterly unworthy of a place in the presence of the Lord Jesus, but Christ answered him, *"Fear not; from henceforth thou shalt catch men"* (Luke 5:10). And when Jesus had said this, *"they forsook all, and followed him"* (Luke 5:11). Now what the Lord said to those disciples He says to us all *"catch men"* (Luke 5:10).

The word "to catch" occurs twice in the New Testament, and means to catch alive. Fishers of fish catch them for death, but fishers of men catch them for life. The other passage where it is found is 2 Timothy 2:26, *"And that they may recover themselves out of the snare of the devil, who are taken captive by him at his will"*. Now that is what fishers of men must do, take others as captives for the Lord Jesus.

From the first chapter of John's Gospel we shall learn how the early disciples went about winning souls for Christ. Let us look into the means which they employed.

How They Fished

1. By public speaking (vv. 35-37): This is possibly the shortest public sermon ever uttered, but it was very fruitful. Since the day that John the Baptist set himself as the example of a public preacher, may thousands have been caught by this method.

2. By personal conversation (vv. 40-46): Neither Andrew nor Philip ever were public men, we read very little about them, but in their humble, more or less private sphere they served the Lord Christ.

   Notice the tact of Philip when he looked up Nathanael. He found him in a very argumentative mood, but he refused to argue with him. He said, *"Come and see"* (v. 39). We have not been sent to argue men to Christ, but to bring men to Christ.

3. By Christ directly (v. 43): No one had any thing to do with the conversion of Philip but the Lord Jesus. Does the Lord still work in this direct way? He does, and we must always be careful not to interfere with this direct work of God, in the soul. The verb to find suggests that it was not an accidental finding, but the result of a search and Philip becomes a follower of Jesus in this. Philip findeth Nathanael.

4. They worked with energy: As we watch these early fishers of men in action we notice an intensity and earnestness about all that they do. John said, *"Behold the Lamb of God"* (v. 29). What he really meant was, "Look earnestly, thoroughly and significantly at the Lamb of God." It is said of Andrew that he brought Peter to Jesus. There is almost a sense of force in this word. It means to lead, and during the trial of our Lord Jesus we have two illustrations as to how this word is used. First, *"Then took they him, and led him, and brought him into the high priest's house"* (Luke 22:54). Second, *"And the whole multitude of them arose, and led him unto Pilate"* (Luke 23:1). The word carries the thought of arresting and leading away. The word indicates that Andrew had to overcome some resistance on Simon's part. Now of Philip we read that he said *"Come and see"* (v. 39). There almost seems to be a combination of the other two expressions here. He uses the very word that John used, and infers, approach Him in my company, and behold Him, look at Him earnestly and significantly, investigate for yourself. This surely was the best way to silence Nathanael's argument.

May we be inspired by the enthusiasm and earnestness of these early disciples as we follow them in fishing for men.

Where They Fished

1. **Among associates** (v. 35): John the Baptist stood that day among his associates and told them of Christ, and we should do likewise. Let us bring our associates to Christ.

2. **Among relatives** (vv. 40-42): Andrew brought his brother. This may be more difficult to do, but we must endeavour to get our loved ones to the Lord Jesus.

3. **Among strangers** (vv. 44-45): Philip was a resident of Bethsaida, and was apparently born in the same city as Andrew and Peter, but Nathanael was of Cana of Galilee (John 21:2). These men lived about twenty miles away from each other, with a lake between them. So if they had ever met before it must have been on very rare occasions. We must seek out sinner even among strangers. We can fish for men anywhere at any time among associates, relatives, or strangers.

Why They Fished

Because of sense of higher spiritual values: Notice what Jesus was to these fishers of men. To John the Baptist He was the Lamb of God; to Andrew He was the Messiah, Christ; and to Philip He was the fulfillment of Old Testament prophets. The testimony of these early disciples arose from what Christ was to them. Out of the abundance of their heart their mouth spoke. Now this is true today. We only witness to Christ in ratio to our appreciation of Christ. It is only as I see Christ my all in all that I truly speak for Him. May we too be possessed by this spirit of higher values, so that we may have deeper consciousness of man's need and danger as well as of God's great remedy.

These Early Fishers of Men

Before we close it might be well for us to look at these men who so wrought for Christ.

THE CHRISTIAN'S AMBITION

1. **Their success:** The names of those who were then won for Christ are given as Andrew, Peter, and Nathanael. As you will see there are two of these that never were very much to the fore-front, but the other became the great apostle to the Circumcision. They all became apostles, but that day, Peter the leader of the little band, was saved. Andrew did not know then that he had landed a whale and not a tiny fish. No one can at the time estimate the great possibilities that lie hidden in those coverts won through human instrumentality.

2. **Their modesty:** John the Baptist was a man of almost measureless spiritual endowment, but these gifts and attainments did not fill him with pride. He was content to call himself only a voice (v. 23). How beautifully the true relation between Christ and His servant is brought before us in the first chapter of John. Our Lord Jesus Christ is the Word (v. 1), but John is merely the voice that utters that Word.

    It is strikingly noticeable throughout this whole Gospel that the apostle John hides himself behind the expression *"one of his disciples, whom Jesus loved"* (John 13:23). There is still another thing mentioned in verse 41 that is very commendable in John. *"He first,"* that is Andrew, *"findeth his own brother Simon"* (v. 41). Andrew was the first to go fishing, and the inference is that Andrew's companion John, did it afterwards by bringing his brother James to Christ. John here takes second place. If the Lord grants us a measure of success we do not need to publish it. Let us ever be ready to publish the success of others, but let our own be in a secondary place.

3. **Their reward:** There is no intimation of reward in this chapter. Now we know from other passages of Scripture that these men will be rewarded, but at this early stage of His public ministry the Lord had not made this known to His disciples. What they

did, they did willingly without the thought of any recompense. It was love to Him that inspired their service. As the apostle Paul unfolds to us our position as ambassadors for Christ in the world, as a prefect to his remarks he says, *"the love of Christ constraineth us"* (2 Cor. 5:14). May the thoughts of that great love constrain us to serve Him the little while we are left down here.

THE RESTORATION OF ISRAEL'S PRIESTHOOD

ZECHARIAH 3:1-10

From Israel the glory of the Lord has departed (Ezek. 10), and this poor backslidden nation is peeled, robbed, and spoiled; nevertheless, God has better things in store for His earthly people, and the day is not far away when He will restore Israel to Himself, and will restore to Israel her former splendour and glory. The message of the Minor Prophets is: the sufferings of Israel and the glory that shall follow.

The prophet Zechariah is much occupied with the restoration of his people and the means that will bring this about.

In chapter one verse eight Christ is seen in the man sitting on the red horse. Red, the colour of blood, is associated with a prancing charger, the figure of power and triumph. The Man Christ Jesus is coming back to earth in power and majesty to triumph over Israel's foes. In 1:18-21 we see that at His return there will be four smiths (instruments of destruction), which will destroy the four horns that have scattered and spoiled poor Israel. The four horns are the Gentiles from the four winds of heaven that have oppressed the Jews. These Gentiles will in turn be punished by God for their hatred of His chosen people.

In chapter 2 the city of Jerusalem is restored, and its population is increased so that it will appear more like London or New York that the city that we know. The metropolitan area of the future city will pass far beyond the present walls, for Jerusalem will be a great city composed of several municipalities: *"Jerusalem shall be inhabited as towns without walls for the multitude of men and cattle therein"* (Zech. 2:4).

Chapter 3 gives us the restoration of the priesthood, as seen in the experience of Joshua the high priest. And at its close there seems to be a suggestion of the rebuilding of the temple, and the laying of the corner stone.

At the opening of the chapter we are introduced to three persons:

1. **Joshua:** That Joshua was a real child of God there is no doubt, as we shall see later on, and he occupied the place of a priest before God and His people. Now this is true of every child of God today. All believers form a holy priesthood to offer sacrifices to God, and a royal priesthood to display the excellencies of Christ to the world (1 Pet. 2:5-9).

   Like Joshua our garments become defiled. His may have been spotted by blood from victims—the stains of death, or covered with dust—the marks of earth. Our contact with the moral dead defiles as does our forced association with the things of the earth; nevertheless, like Joshua we can stand before the Lord, and there find cleansing.

2. **Satan:** we know this one, his name is Adversary, for he is the accuser of the brethren (Rev. 12:10), and he is ready to accuse poor Joshua, and resist any effort to restore him.

3. **The Lord:**

   (a) He rebukes Satan: No mere man can do that, nor can the highest order of angels. Michael, the archangel when he contended with the devil over the body of Moses—for because of the claims of death that body should have fallen into corruption, but apparently was delivered from it by the interposition of Michael (Deut. 34:5,6; Jude 9; Luke 9:30,31) said, *"The Lord rebuke thee"* (Jude 9).

   (b) He acknowledged Joshua as His child: *"is not this a brand plucked out of the fire?"* (v. 2). He did not say, "Is not this a brand that I am going to pluck out of the fire." The words of the Lord do not point to something that He was about to do, but rather to what He had already done, and He here acknowledged this defiled man to be one that He had delivered from the fires of judgement. How gracious of God! This alone should soften our hearts, to think that although we backslide and become defiled, our Lord, even in the presence of the adversary that accuses us, is willing, not to disown us, but to acknowledge us as His.

4. **Joshua restored:** There was no change in the style of his clothing, but there was a change in the condition of his clothing. He was a priest before this experience, and he was still a priest. The difference is this, He was a priest contaminated by sin, but now he is a priest cleansed from all sin, and this cleansing was effected by God in His own divine presence. This is still God's way. We cannot cleanse ourselves, but if in His presence *"we confess our sins, he is faithful and just to forgive us our sins, and to cleanse us from all unrighteousness"* (1 John 1:9).

5. **Joshua reinstated:** Joshua is now to be reinstated as the leader of God's household, and the keeper of God's tabernacle, but his reinstatement depends upon his behaviour.

   (a) **The precept:** *"if thou wilt keep my charge"* (v. 7).

   (b) **The practice:** *"If thou wilt walk in my ways"* (v.7).

   When we, as the people of God, have wandered away from Him, and have failed in our service for Him, there is only one sure way back again into usefulness, and that is by following in daily practice the precepts laid down in His blessed Word.

   (c) **The promise:** *" I will give thee places to walk among these that stand by"* (v. 7). What group is meant by those that stand by?

   It is difficult to say, but who ever they were when they saw the behaviour of Joshua they placed such perfect confidence in him that he was able to move in and out among them with perfect acceptance.

"When a man's ways please the Lord, he maketh even his enemies to be at peace with him" (Prov. 16:7). When a man's ways please the Lord he will find that his brethren will not look with suspicion on him but with confidence. The dying prayer of Moses for Asher was *"let him be acceptable to his brethren"* (Deut. 33:24).

6. **Symbol men:** Joshua, the high priest and his fellows —the entire priesthood are spoken of as men that are a sign or symbol for that is the meaning of the words "men wondered at." What were they a sign or symbol of? The coming of God's Servant—the Branch.

We are called upon to live in an entirely different dispensation, but we should so live before the world that our manner and testimony will be a sign to those who know us of this Coming again of the Lord Jesus.

Unless You Repent
by H. A. Ironside

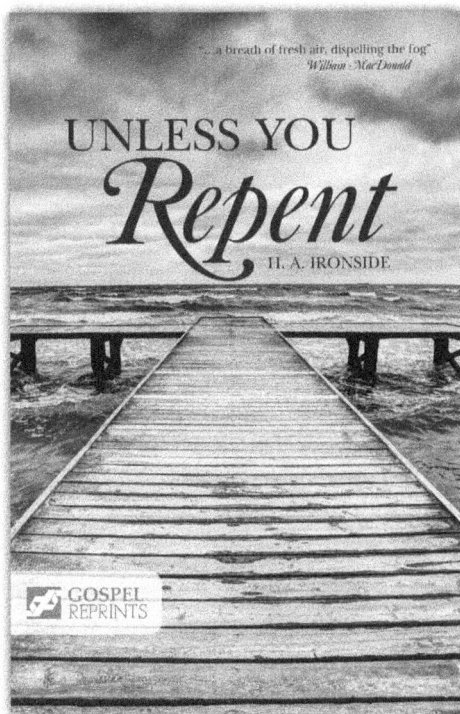

"It is especially timely that this book should be reprinted at this time. It deals with issues that are the subject of some misinformation and misunderstanding. Ironside's clear and gracious handling of the much misunderstood doctrine of repentance comes as a breath of fresh air, dispelling the fog."

—William MacDonald

9781882701070 • Paperback • 164 pages
Published by Gospel Folio Press